TREASURY OF LITERATURE

HOLD ON TIGHT

SENIOR AUTHORS
ROGER C. FARR
DOROTHY S. STRICKLAND

AUTHORS
RICHARD F. ABRAHAMSON
ELLEN BOOTH CHURCH
BARBARA BOWEN COULTER
BERNICE E. CULLINAN
MARGARET A. GALLEGO
W. DORSEY HAMMOND
JUDITH L. IRVIN
KAREN KUTIPER
DONNA M. OGLE
TIMOTHY SHANAHAN
PATRICIA SMITH
JUNKO YOKOTA
HALLIE KAY YOPP

SENIOR CONSULTANTS
ASA G. HILLIARD III
JUDY M. WALLIS

CONSULTANTS
ALONZO A. CRIM
ROLANDO R. HINOJOSA-SMITH
LEE BENNETT HOPKINS
ROBERT J. STERNBERG

HARCOURT BRACE & COMPANY
Orlando Atlanta Austin Boston San Francisco Chicago Dallas New York
Toronto London

Acknowledgments

For permission to reprint copyrighted material, grateful acknowledgment is made to the following sources:

Bordas, Paris, France: Cover illustration by Ye Xin from *On the Other Side of the World* by Michèle Kahn. © 1987 by Bordas. Originally published in France under the title *L'autre bout du monde.*

Bradbury Press, an Affiliate of Macmillan Publishing Company, Inc.: "The Snow Glory" from *Henry and Mudge in Puddle Trouble* by Cynthia Rylant, illustrated by Sucie Stevenson. Text copyright © 1987 by Cynthia Rylant; illustrations copyright © 1987 by Suçie Stevenson.

CELTA Amaquemecan: Cover illustration by Martha Avilés from *I Like Storybooks* by Liliana Santirso. Illustration © 1991 by Martha Avilés. Originally published in Spanish under the title *Me gustan los libros de cuentos,* Amecameca, Mexico.

Childrens Press: Cover illustration from *So That's How the Moon Changes Shape!* by Allan Fowler. Cover photographs courtesy of Yerkes Observatory Photograph.

Dial Books for Young Readers, a division of Penguin Books USA Inc.: *There's An Alligator Under My Bed* by Mercer Mayer. Copyright © 1987 by Mercer Mayer. *Peace at Last* by Jill Murphy. Copyright © 1980 by Jill Murphy.

Aileen Fisher: "Dreams" from *Up the Windy Hill* by Aileen Fisher. Copyright renewed. Published by Abelard Press, New York, 1953.

Four Winds Press, a division of Macmillan Publishing Company: Cover illustration by Jennifer Northway from *Carry Go Bring Come* by Vyanne Samuels. Illustration copyright © 1988 by Jennifer Northway.

Greenwillow Books, a division of William Morrow & Company, Inc.: Cover illustration from *The Quilt* by Ann Jonas. Copyright © 1984 by Ann Jonas. "I'm Awake, I'm Awake!" from *My Parents Think I'm Sleeping* by Jack Prelutsky. Text copyright © 1985 by Jack Prelutsky.

Harcourt Brace & Company: Cover illustration from *Growing Vegetable Soup* by Lois Ehlert. Copyright © 1987 by Lois Ehlert. Cover illustration from *Moon Rope* by Lois Ehlert, translated by Amy Prince. Illustration copyright © 1992 by Lois Ehlert.

HarperCollins Publishers: Cover illustration from *I Want to Be an Astronaut* by Byron Barton. Copyright © 1988 by Byron Barton. "Tommy" from *Bronzeville Boys and Girls* by Gwendolyn Brooks. Text copyright © 1956 by Gwendolyn Brooks Blakely. Cover illustration by Pat Cummings from *Just Us Women* by Jeannette Caines. Illustration copyright © 1982 by Pat Cummings. Illustration by Robin Spowart from "Oh Where, Oh Where Has My Little Dog Gone?" in *Songs from Mother Goose,* compiled by Nancy Larrick. Illustration copyright © 1989 by Robin Spowart. "Little Seeds" from *The Winds that Come from Far Away* by Else Holmelund Minarik. Text copyright © 1964 by Else Holmelund Minarik. Cover illustration from *Caps For Sale* by Esphyr Slobodkina. Copyright © 1940, 1947, renewed © 1968 by Esphyr Slobodkina.

Houghton Mifflin Company: *Jamaica's Find* by Juanita Havill, illustrated by Anne Sibley O'Brien. Text copyright © 1986 by Juanita Havill; illustrations copyright © 1986 by Anne Sibley O'Brien.

Little, Brown and Company: *Lost!* by David McPhail. Copyright © 1990 by David McPhail.

Macmillan Publishing Company, a division of Macmillan, Inc.: *Dreams* by Ezra Jack Keats. Copyright © 1974 by Ezra Jack Keats.

William Morrow & Company, Inc.: "Good Night" from *Vacation Time* by Nikki Giovanni. Text copyright © 1980 by Nikki Giovanni.

Marian Reiner, on behalf of Eve Merriam: "Lights in the Dark" from *A Poem for a Pickle* by Eve Merriam. Text copyright © 1989 by Eve Merriam.

Elizabeth Roach: "Sleeping Outdoors" from *Rhymes About Us* by Marchette Chute. Text copyright 1974 by E. P. Dutton Co.

Seymour Simon: From *Silly Animal Jokes and Riddles* by Seymour Simon. Text copyright © 1980 by Seymour Simon.

Tambourine Books, a division of William Morrow & Company, Inc.: *Henny Penny* by Stephen Butler. Copyright © 1991 by Stephen Butler.

Troll Associates, Mahwah, NJ: From *All About Seeds* by Susan Kuchalla. Text copyright © 1982 by Troll Associates. *Stars* by Roy Wandelmaier, illustrated by Irene Trivas. Copyright © 1985 by Troll Associates.

Rose Wyler: From *What Happens If?: Science Experiments You Can Do By Yourself* (Retitled: "Shadow Pictures") by Rose Wyler. Text copyright © by Rose Wyler.

continued on page 204

Dear Reader,

Hold on tight and get ready for a wonderful ride. In this book you will meet a bear who takes a trip to the stars. You will also meet Roberto, a boy who saves a cat. See what happens when a bear gets lost in the city and when Jamaica finds a toy dog. Meet people from many different places. All have something wonderful to share.

Ready, set, turn the page. Hold on for the ride!

Sincerely,
The Authors

Unit One
In the Night / 8

UNIT TWO
On Our Way / 92

Unit One

In the Night

"Girls and boys, come out to play,
The moon is shining bright as day."

Mother Goose

What do you dream about at
night? Wait until you see the
wood carvings that the artists
of Mexico dreamed up! As
you read these nighttime stories,
think of all the wonderful things
you can see in the night.

T H E M E S

BOOKSHELF

THE QUILT
by Ann Jonas

A young girl has a new quilt. Her mother and father made it for her from scraps of such things as her baby pajamas and her first curtains. The first time she sleeps under it, she has an exciting dream!
Harcourt Brace Library Book

SO THAT'S HOW THE MOON CHANGES SHAPE!
by Allan Fowler

Does the moon really change its shape? Can people, animals, and plants live on the moon? Find out by reading this book.
Harcourt Brace Library Book

10

I Want to Be an Astronaut

by Byron Barton

3-2-1-0 Blast-off! Zoom into space with this shuttle crew. Take a space walk. Fix a satellite. Find out what it's like to be an astronaut!

ALA Notable Book

Moon Rope / Un lazo a la luna

by Lois Ehlert

Fox wants to go to the moon. Mole agrees to go with him. Will they really get to the moon? What will happen along the way?

Award-Winning Author

On the Other Side of the World

by Michèle Kahn

Do you like bedtime stories? So do children all over the world! In faraway Japan you will meet a friend who is a lot like you!

THEME

I Can't Sleep

What do you do to help you sleep? Read about things others do when they can't sleep!

CONTENTS

PEACE AT LAST

by Jill Murphy

The hour was late.

Mr. Bear was tired, Mrs. Bear

was tired, and Baby Bear was tired,

so they all went to bed.

Mrs. Bear fell asleep.
Mr. Bear didn't.
Mrs. Bear began to snore.
"SNORE," went Mrs. Bear.
"SNORE, SNORE, SNORE."
"Oh, NO!" said Mr. Bear,
"I can't stand THIS."
So he got up and went to
sleep in Baby Bear's room.

Baby Bear was not asleep either.

He was lying in bed, pretending

to be an airplane.

"NYAAOW!" went Baby Bear.

"NYAAOW! NYAAOW!"

"Oh, NO!" said Mr. Bear,

"I can't stand THIS."

So he got up

and went to sleep in the living room.

TICK-TOCK . . . went the living room
clock. . . . TICK-TOCK, TICK-TOCK,
CUCKOO! CUCKOO!
"Oh, NO!" said Mr. Bear,
"I can't stand THIS."
So he went off to sleep in the kitchen.

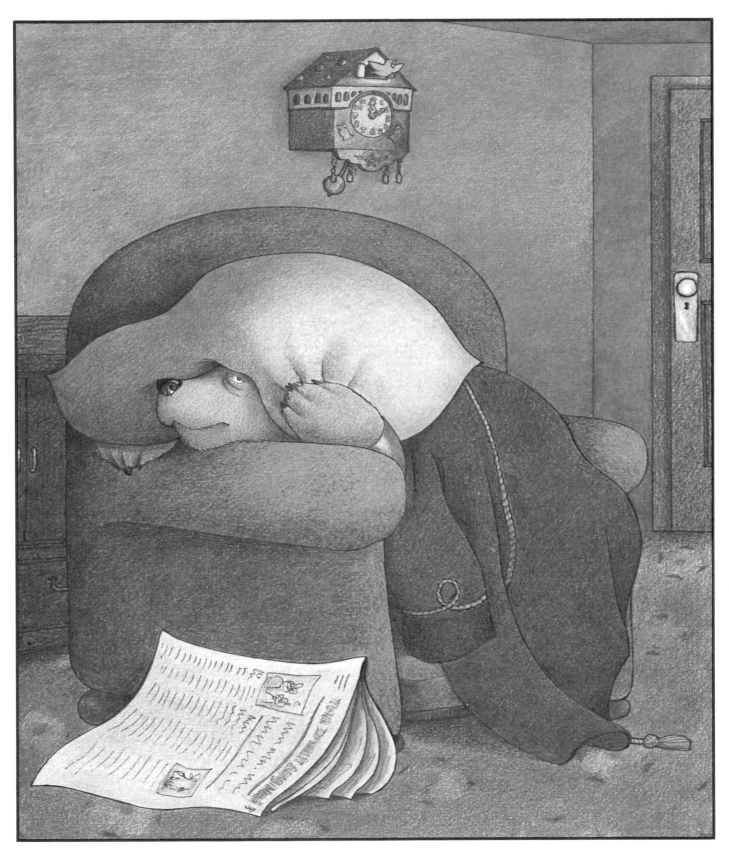

19

DRIP, DRIP . . . went the leaky
kitchen faucet.
HMMMMMMMMMMM . . .
went the refrigerator.
"Oh, NO," said Mr. Bear,
"I can't stand THIS."
So he got up
and went to sleep in the garden.

21

Well, you would not believe
what noises there are in
the garden at night.
"TOO-WHIT-TOO-WHOO!"
went the owl.
"SNUFFLE, SNUFFLE," went
the hedgehog.
"MIAAAOW!" sang the cats
on the wall.
"Oh, NO!" said Mr. Bear,
"I can't stand THIS."
So he went off to sleep in
the car.

23

It was cold in the car
and uncomfortable, but
Mr. Bear was so tired
that he didn't notice.
He was just falling asleep
when all the birds started to
sing and the sun peeped in at
the window.
"TWEET TWEET!" went the birds.
SHINE, SHINE . . . went the sun.
"Oh, NO!" said Mr. Bear,
"I can't stand THIS."
So he got up and went back
into the house.

24

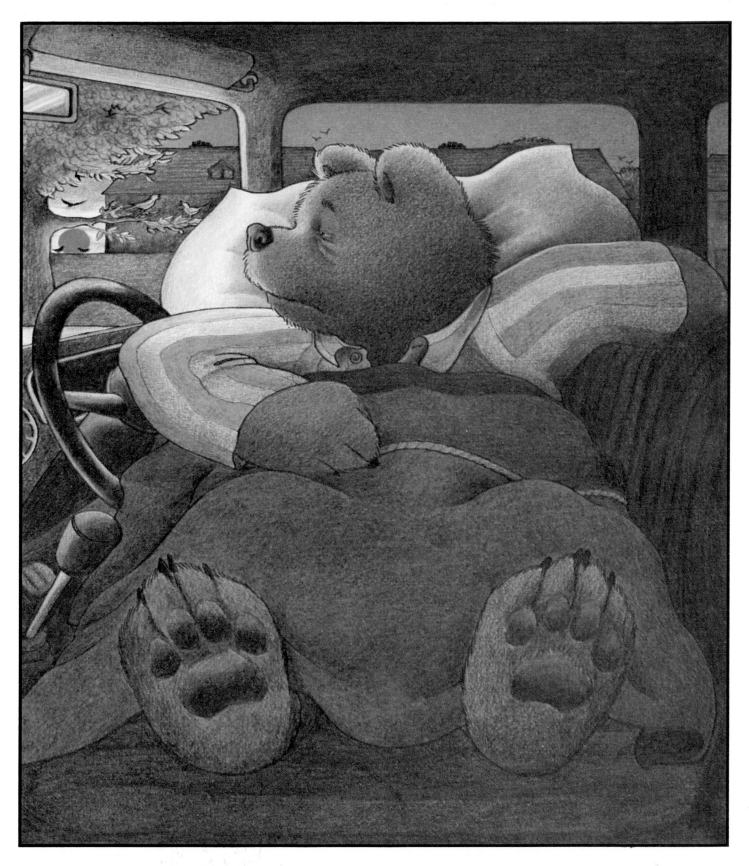

In the house Baby Bear was
fast asleep, and Mrs. Bear had
turned over and wasn't snoring
anymore.

Mr. Bear got into bed and closed
his eyes.

"Peace at last," he said to himself.

BRRRRRRRRRRRRRR . . . went the
alarm clock. BRRRRRR!

Mrs. Bear sat up and rubbed her eyes.

"Good morning, dear," she said.

"Did you sleep well?"

"Not VERY well, dear," yawned Mr. Bear.

"Never mind," said Mrs. Bear. "I'll

bring you the mail and a nice cup of tea."

"And she did."

🐻 What part of the story did you think was the funniest? Why?

🐻 What else could Mr. Bear have done to get some sleep?

WRITE   What do you do when you can't sleep? Write a list of things to do when you can't get to sleep.

I'M AWAKE! I'M AWAKE!

by Jack Prelutsky

I'm awake! I'm awake!
I cannot shut my eyes,
I'm unable to sleep,
though I've made many tries,

I'm sure I've explored
every inch of my bed,
my body's exhausted,
and so is my head.

I wiggle, I fidget,
I tumble, I twist,
I pound my poor pillow
with fist after fist,

I stopped counting sheep
when I reached ninety-three.
I'm awake! I'm awake!
I cannot fall asleeeeeeeeeeeeeee

Illustrated by Jackie Snider

30

GOOD NIGHT
by Nikki Giovanni

Goodnight Mommy
Goodnight Dad

I kiss them as I go

Goodnight Teddy
Goodnight Spot

The moonbeams call me so

I climb the stairs
Go down the hall
And walk into my room

My day of play is ending
But my night of sleep's in bloom

LIGHTS IN THE DARK

by Eve Merriam

In the quiet
of the night,
shining,
shining,
shining bright.

Emerald stars
or fireflies?

Cat's eyes,
cat's eyes,
cat's eyes.

DREAMS
by Aileen Fisher

Do you ever
wonder too
what dreams do
when they
are through?

Illustrated by
Jackie Snider

33

Jack Prelutsky's silly rhyming poems about people and animals have been making people laugh for years. He often visits schools. There he reads his poems for children, plays the guitar, and sings.

Aileen Fisher grew up on a farm. As a child she liked to take long walks in the woods. There she learned to love animals and the outdoors. Her poems make us wonder about nature and everyday things.

Illustrated by
Jackie Snider

Eve Merriam's poems are about things children like. Her poetry seems to ask the reader to join in the fun! Some of her poems are about bugs, animals, stars, and wishes.

Nikki Giovanni writes poems about people for children and adults. She writes about feelings children have, such as happiness and sadness. Some of her poems are about happy times she had as a child. Nikki Giovanni hopes that her poems will help people to understand one another better.

Dreams

CHILDREN'S CHOICE

EZRA JACK KEATS

It was hot.

After supper Roberto came
to his window to talk with Amy.

"Look what I made in school today—
a paper mouse!"

"Does it do anything?" Amy asked.

Roberto thought for a while.

"I don't know," he said. Then he put
the mouse on the window sill.

37

As it grew darker, the city got quieter.
"Bedtime, Roberto," called his mother.
"Bedtime for you, too,"
other mothers called.
"Good-night, Amy."
"Good-night, Roberto."
"G-o-o-o-o-d-night!" echoed the parrot.
Soon they were all in bed.

Someone began to dream.
Soon everybody was dreaming—
except one person.
Somehow Roberto just couldn't
fall asleep. It got later and later.

41

Finally he got up
and went to the window.
What he saw down in the street
made him gasp!
There was Archie's cat!
A big dog had chased him into a box.
The dog snarled.
"He's trapped!" thought Roberto.
"What should I do?"

Then it happened!
His pajama sleeve
brushed the paper mouse
off the window sill.
It sailed away from him.

Down it fell,
turning this way
and that, casting a big shadow
on the wall.
The shadow grew bigger—
and bigger—

and BIGGER!

The dog howled and ran away.

The cat dashed across the street
and jumped through Archie's open window.

"Wow! Wait till I tell Archie what
happened!" thought Roberto.

"That was some mouse!"

He yawned and went back to bed.

Morning came, and everybody
was getting up.
Except one person.
Roberto was fast asleep,
dreaming.

How did this story make you
feel? Tell why.

How did Roberto save
Archie's cat?

WRITE   What will Roberto tell
Archie? What will Archie say?
Write what the boys will say to
each other.

What happened when Roberto's paper mouse fell out the window? That's right! The mouse's shadow could be seen on the wall. You can make shadows, too.

SHADOW

by Rose Wyler

illustrated by Jackie Snider

Put a flashlight on a table. Hold your hand in front of the light. Now walk to the wall. What happens to the shadow? Does it stay the same size?

At first the shadow is big. Your hand is near the flashlight and blocks a lot of light.

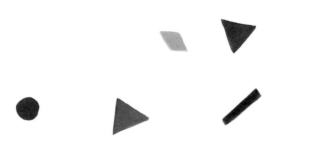

PICTURES

As you walk to the wall, your hand blocks less and less light. The shadow gets smaller and smaller. When your hand is near the wall, the shadow is smallest of all.

Now make some shadow pictures. To make a duck, hold your hand this way. Make your fingers go up and down. The duck will talk.

Try making some other shadow pictures like this.

rabbit

cat

butterfly

horse

Can you make up a story about these shadow pictures?
Ask your friends to help you. Then put on a shadow show.

I Can't Sleep

How are Mr. Bear and Roberto alike?

Who do you think feels happier in the morning, Mr. Bear or Roberto? What makes you think that?

WRITER'S WORKSHOP

Think about night at home. Draw a picture. Show what you do before you go to bed. Write a story about your picture.

THEME

Starry Night

What do you know about stars?
Have you ever slept under the stars?
You can read and learn about
the stars!

CONTENTS

55

S·T·A·R·S

by Roy Wandelmaier
illustrated by Irene Trivas

It is day. Can you see a bright star?

Yes, you can! The sun is a star.

The bright sun is so close to us.

It outshines all the other stars.

Now it is night. Look up.
Look at the other stars.

All the other stars seem small.
That is because they are so far away.

But many stars are bigger than our sun.
They are called red giants.

Some stars are smaller than our sun.
They are called dwarfs.

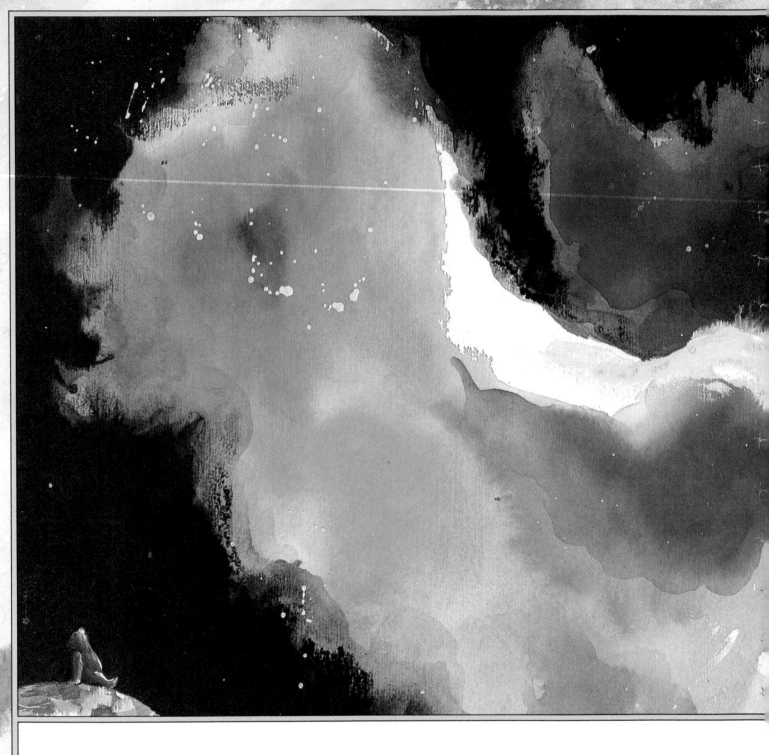

How does a star begin?
When gas and dust in space come together,
a star is born!

Let's take a trip to the stars.

A star glows hot. A star glows bright.

Are all stars as hot as our sun? Some are even hotter!

The hottest stars give off blue light.
Cooler stars give off red light.

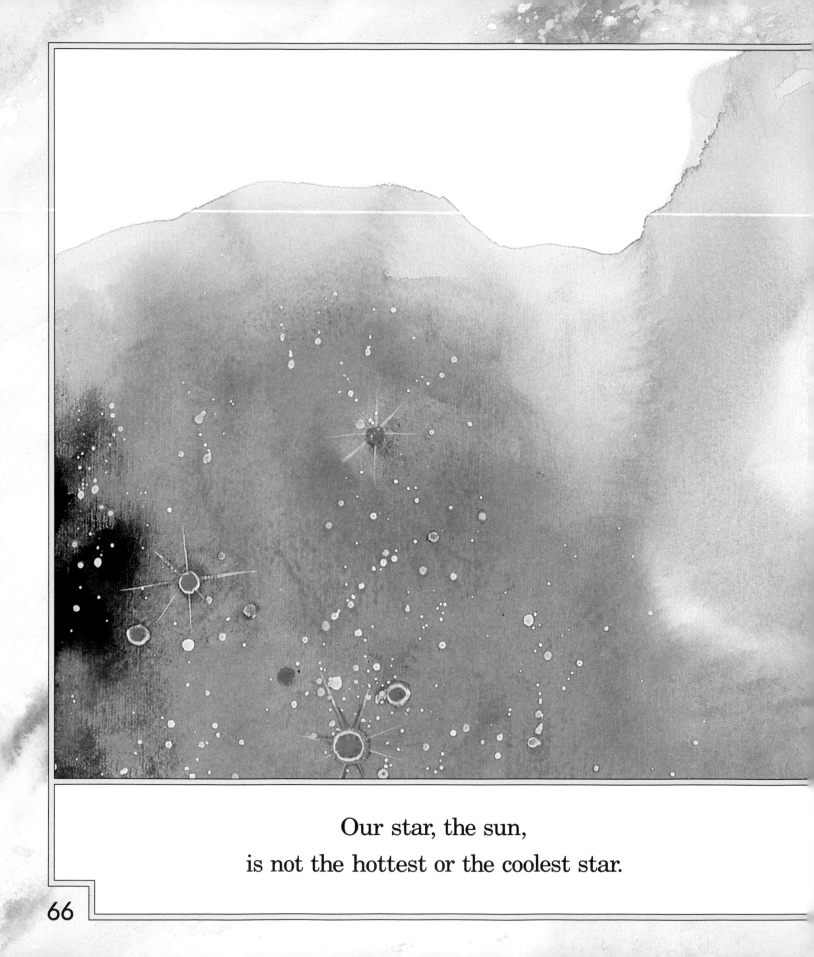

Our star, the sun,
is not the hottest or the coolest star.

It is in the middle.

It shines yellow.

After some stars live a long time,
they explode. We call this a supernova.

The exploded gas goes out into space.

And some of it may be used to make a new star.

Stars are so far away.
But stars are close enough to shine for us.
Watch for them tonight.

 What surprised you the most about this story?

 What new things did you learn about stars?

WRITE Would you like to take a trip to the stars? Write about why you would or would not want to go.

SLEEPING OUTDOORS

by Marchette Chute

illustrated by Kathy Lengyel

Under the dark is a star,
Under the star is a tree,
Under the tree is a blanket,
And under the blanket is me.

Starry Night

Imagine that you could give the sun a new name. What would you name it?

If you were sleeping outdoors on a starry night, what would you do?

WRITER'S WORKSHOP

Draw a picture. Show yourself taking a walk at nighttime. What do you see? What do you hear? Write about your picture.

THEME

In My Room

Do you like to sleep in your room at night? Read a funny story about a boy who finds something strange in his room. What will he do?

CONTENTS

THERE'S AN ALLIGATOR UNDER MY BED
written and illustrated by
Mercer Mayer

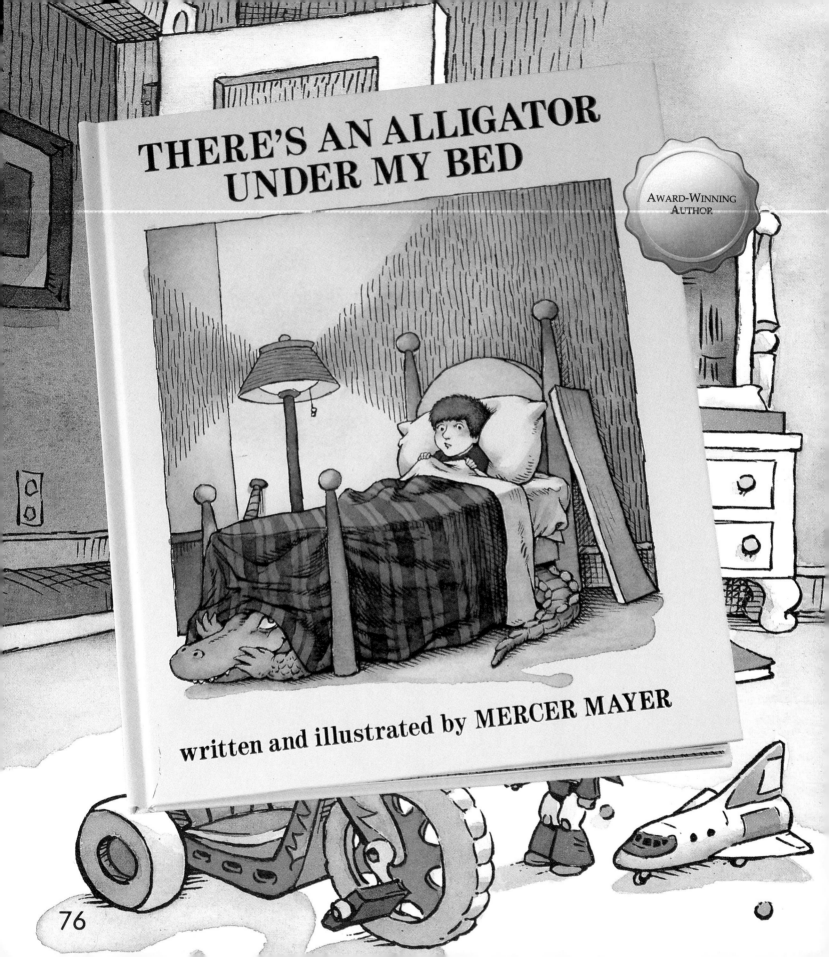

THERE'S AN ALLIGATOR
UNDER MY BED

AWARD-WINNING
AUTHOR

written and illustrated by MERCER MAYER

There used to be an alligator under my bed.
When it was time to go to sleep,
I had to be very careful

because I knew he was there.
But whenever I looked,
he hid . . . or something.

So I'd call Mom and Dad.
But they never saw it.
It was up to me.
I just had to do something
about that alligator.

So I went to the kitchen
to get some alligator bait.
I filled a paper bag full
of things alligators like to eat.
I put a peanut butter sandwich,
some fruit, and the last piece
of pie in the garage.

I put cookies down the hall.

82

I left fresh vegetables on the stairs.

I put a soda and some candy next to my bed.
Then I watched and waited.
Sure enough, out he came to get
something to eat.
Then I hid in the hall closet.

I followed him down the stairs.
I followed him down the hall.

When he crawled into the garage,
I slammed the door and locked it.

Then I went to bed.
There wasn't even any mess to clean up.

Now that there is an alligator in the garage,
I wonder if my dad will have any trouble
getting in his car tomorrow morning.
I'll just leave him a note.

🦎 What part of the story did you like the best?

🦎 How do you know that this story could not really
  happen?

WRITE What might happen in the morning when
the boy's father goes into the garage? Write about it.

In My Room

Do you think the boy's idea was a good one? Tell why or why not.

Why didn't his parents believe him?

WRITER'S WORKSHOP

Imagine that you find something under your bed. What is it? What do you do? Write a story. Draw a picture to go with it.

CONNECTIONS

Multicultural Connection

Artists of Mexico

What do you dream about at night? Have you ever dreamed about animals like the ones in these pictures? Artists get ideas from nighttime dreams and from daydreams, too.

Artists in Mexico make these wonderful figures. They cut them out of wood. Then they paint them bright colors. Colorful figures like these can be found in many museums.

Draw your own dream animal. Paint it many colors.

Social Studies Connection
Artists

There are many kinds of artists in the world. Go to the library. Find a book about artists from other countries. Bring the book to class, and share what you learn.

Science Connection
Nighttime Animals

Many animals sleep during the day and are awake at night. Name some of these animals. Draw a picture of one, and tell what it does at night.

Unit Two

On Our Way

Where do you like to go? What do you like to see on your way? What would you like to be when you grow up? Jo Ann Jeong dreamed of being a park ranger and made her dream come true. As you read these stories, think about the dreams that might come true for you along your way.

THEMES

GROWING VEGETABLE SOUP

by Lois Ehlert

How can you grow vegetable soup? This book tells, step by step. It may take a while, but you can do it!

Award-Winning Author

Harcourt Brace Library Book

CARRY GO BRING COME

by Vyanne Samuels

Leon's sister is getting married today. Many people are telling him what to do. Find out what silly thing happens to Leon.

Harcourt Brace Library Book

Just Us Women

by Jeannette Caines

Join a girl and her aunt as they go on a trip together. See how much fun they have on the road.

Award-Winning Author

Caps For Sale

by Esphyr Slobodkina

"Caps! Caps for Sale!" shouts the peddler. But something happens when the peddler takes a nap. Watch out for monkey business when you read this story!

Award-Winning Author

I Like Storybooks

by Liliana Santirso and Martha Avilés

Would you like to be a superhero? Would you like to fly through space and time? Hold on tight when you read this book. It will take you to many places!

95

THEME

Signs of Spring

Do you like spring? Here are some stories and poems about things that grow in spring.

CONTENTS

The Snow Glory

When the snow melted and Spring came,
Henry and his big dog Mudge stayed
outside all the time.

Henry had missed riding his bike.
Mudge had missed chewing on sticks.
They were glad it was warmer.

One day when Henry and Mudge were in their yard, Henry saw something blue on the ground.

He got closer to it.

"Mudge!" he called. "It's a flower!"

Mudge slowly walked over and sniffed the blue flower.

Then he sneezed all over Henry.

"Aw, Mudge," Henry said.

Later, Henry's mother told him that the flower was called a snow glory.

"Can I pick it?" Henry asked.

"Oh, no," said his mother. "Let it grow."

So Henry didn't pick it.

Every day he saw the snow glory in
the yard, blue and looking so pretty.
    He knew he shouldn't pick it.
    He was trying not to pick it.
    But he thought how nice it would look
in a jar.

He thought how nice to bring it inside.

He thought how nice it would be to own that snow glory.

Every day he stood with Mudge and looked at the flower.

Mudge would stick his nose into the grass all around the snow glory.

But he never looked at it the way Henry did.

"Don't you think the snow glory has
been growing long enough?" Henry
would ask his mother.

"Let it grow, Henry," she would say.

Oh, Henry wanted that snow glory.
And one day he just knew he had to
have it.

So he took Mudge by the collar and he
stood beside the snow glory.

"I'm going to pick it," Henry whispered to Mudge.

"I've let it grow a long time."

Henry bent his head and he said in Mudge's ear, "Now I *need* it."

And Mudge wagged his tail, licked Henry's face, then put his big mouth right over that snow glory . . .

and he ate it.

"*No, Mudge!*" Henry said.

But too late.

There was a blue flower in Mudge's belly.

"I said *need* it, not *eat* it!" shouted Henry.

He was so mad because Mudge took his flower.

It was Henry's flower and Mudge took it.

And Henry almost said, "Bad dog," but he stopped.

He looked at Mudge, who looked back at him with soft brown eyes and a flower in his belly.

Henry knew it wasn't his snow glory.

He knew it wasn't anybody's snow glory.

Just a thing to let grow.

And if someone ate it, it was just a thing to let go.

Henry stopped feeling mad.

He put his arms around Mudge's big head.

"Next time, Mudge," he said, "try to *listen* better."

Mudge wagged his tail and licked his lips.

One blue petal fell from his mouth into Henry's hand.

Henry smiled, put it in his pocket, and they went inside.

Does Henry remind you of anyone you know? Tell about that person.

Why do you think Henry didn't stay mad at Mudge?

WRITE Imagine that Mudge can talk. Write what he might say about why he ate the snow glory.

Tommys

I put a seed into the ground
And said, "I'll watch it grow."
I watered it and cared for it
As well as I could know.

One day I walked in my back yard,
And oh, what did I see!
My seed had popped itself right out,
Without consulting me.

by Gwendolyn Brooks

LITTLE SEEDS

Little seeds we sow in spring,
growing while the robins sing,
give us carrots, peas and beans,
tomatoes, pumpkins, squash and greens.

And we pick them,
one and all,
through the summer,
through the fall.

Winter comes, then spring, and then
little seeds we sow again.

by Else Holmelund Minarik

illustrated by Tracy Sabin

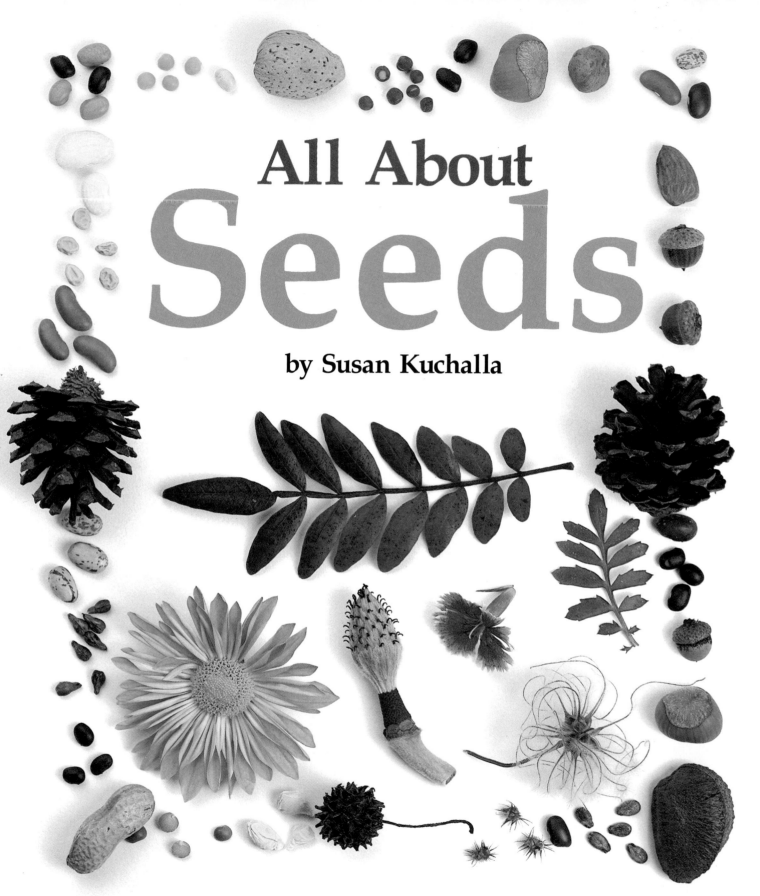

All About
Seeds

by Susan Kuchalla

What is a seed?
An acorn is a seed. A pine
cone holds seeds. A seed
can be a pit or a nut or
a bean.

115

Do you know what grows from a seed?
Plants grow from seeds. A flower is a
plant. A bush is a plant, and
so is a tree.

Do you know how seeds are planted?
Sometimes they just fall to the ground.
Sometimes they are carried and planted
by the wind.

Sometimes they are carried and planted by water. Sometimes they are planted by animals. And sometimes they are planted by people.

Seeds need water to grow. Rain gives them water. Or people can bring water to them.

Seeds also need air and sunshine. The sun warms
the ground. The seed starts to grow. There is a
little plant in the seed. It grows and grows. Soon
the stem pushes up, and leaves grow.
Leaves reach out for sunlight. Plants make their
own food. The plant grows bigger and stronger.

What kind of plant will it be?

It might be a flower. It might be
a fruit or a vegetable. It might be
a pine tree. It might be a tree
that is covered with fruit.

But this plant grew from an acorn . . .

. . . so it will grow into a mighty oak tree!

🌿 What did you learn about seeds?

🌿 What kind of seed would you like to plant? How would you take care of it?

WRITE   Imagine that you must teach a friend how to grow a plant. Write five things you would tell your friend to do.

Signs of Spring

How do you think the snow glory grew?

What would Henry want to tell Tommy about the seed that popped out?

WRITER'S WORKSHOP

Think about things that grow in spring. What plant would you grow? Write how you would grow it. Draw a picture to show your plant.

125

THEME

Silly Journeys

What's so funny? Read about some silly animals and the silly trips they take!

CONTENTS

HENNY PENNY

adapted from a retelling by Stephen Butler

Characters

Narrator	Cocky Locky	Goosey Loosey
Henny Penny	Ducky Lucky	Turkey Lurkey
	Foxy Loxy	

Narrator: One day while Henny Penny was sitting beneath the oak tree an acorn fell and hit her on the head.

Henny Penny: Goodness me! The sky is falling! I must go and tell the king.

Narrator: So Henny Penny ran off in a great hurry to tell the king the sky was falling. She had not gone far before she met Cocky Locky.

Cocky Locky: Where are you going,
Henny Penny?

Henny Penny: Oh, Cocky Locky! The sky is
falling! And I am going to tell the king.

Cocky Locky: Goodness me! I'll come with you.

Narrator: So Henny Penny and Cocky Locky
hurried on to tell the king the sky was falling.
They had not gone far before they met
Ducky Lucky.

Ducky Lucky: Where are you two going?

Cocky Locky: Oh, Ducky Lucky! The sky is falling! And we are going to tell the king.

Ducky Lucky: Goodness me! I'll come with you.

Narrator: So Henny Penny, Cocky Locky, and Ducky Lucky hurried on to tell the king the sky was falling. They had not gone far before they met Goosey Loosey.

Goosey Loosey: Where are you all going?

Ducky Lucky: Oh, Goosey Loosey! The sky is falling! And we are going to tell the king.

Goosey Loosey: Goodness me! I'll come with you.

Narrator: So Henny Penny, Cocky Locky, Ducky Lucky, and Goosey Loosey hurried on to tell the king the sky was falling. They had not gone far before they met Turkey Lurkey.

Turkey Lurkey: Where are you all going?

Goosey Loosey: Oh, Turkey Lurkey! The sky is falling! And we are going to tell the king.

Turkey Lurkey: Goodness me! I'll come with you.

Narrator: So Henny Penny, Cocky Locky, Ducky Lucky, Goosey Loosey, and Turkey Lurkey hurried on to tell the king the sky was falling. Suddenly Foxy Loxy appeared.

Foxy Loxy: And where are you all going in such a hurry?

All Birds: Oh, Foxy Loxy! The sky is falling! We are going to tell the king.

Foxy Loxy: But you're going the wrong way! The king's palace is *that* way.

Narrator: Foxy Loxy pointed to a path leading into the woods. So Henny Penny, Cocky Locky, Ducky Lucky, Goosey Loosey, and Turkey Lurkey hurried down the path. They ran on and on until at last they reached the king's palace.

Foxy Loxy: Come in and tell me your story, Henny Penny.

Narrator: But as Henny Penny curtsied, she saw a bushy red tail beneath the king's robe.

Henny Penny: It's a trap! Run!

Narrator: Foxy Loxy threw off his cunning disguise and sprang to the door.

Foxy Loxy: Surprise! I'm going to eat you all for dinner.

Narrator: Henny Penny woke up with a start and opened her eyes. She was still trembling.

Henny Penny: Goodness me! I must have been dreaming.

Narrator: But just then an acorn fell and hit her on the head.

Henny Penny: Goodness me! The sky is falling! I must go and tell the king.

 Would you like to have Henny Penny
as a friend? Why or why not?

 How did you know that the story was
just Henny Penny's dream?

WRITE Imagine that you are Ducky Lucky. You
want to tell Henny Penny that the sky is not really
falling. Write what you will say.

144

Silly Journeys

Why was Henny Penny's trip to see the king silly?

Which do you think is funnier, "Henny Penny" or one of the jokes? Why?

WRITER'S WORKSHOP

Pretend you are in "Henny Penny." Henny Penny tells you the sky is falling. Write what you would say to her.

146

THEME

Lost and Found

Have you ever found something?
What was it? Read to see what is
"Lost and Found"!

CONTENTS

I am walking down the street when I hear
someone crying.

It's a bear!

He looks lost and afraid.

The tall buildings scare him.

And he's never seen so many people.

"Don't worry," I tell him.

"The buildings won't hurt you, and

most of the people are friendly.

How did you get here?" I ask.

"I climbed in to have a nap,"

he explains, "and when I woke up,

I was *lost!*"

"I'll help you. Tell me where you live."

"There are trees where I live," he tells me.

So we find some trees.

"More trees," he says, "and water!"

I take him to a place where there are more

trees—and water, too.

"No," he says. "This is not it either."

I have an idea. "Follow me!" I say.

I take him to a tall building.

We go inside, get on the elevator, and ride all

the way to the top.

From up here we can see the whole city.

"Look!" I say. "Now we can find your home."

"There it is!" he says, pointing.

Down we go, across three streets
and into the park.
The park is not the bear's home
after all—but he likes it there.
We go for a boat ride,
we have lunch,
and we go to the playground.

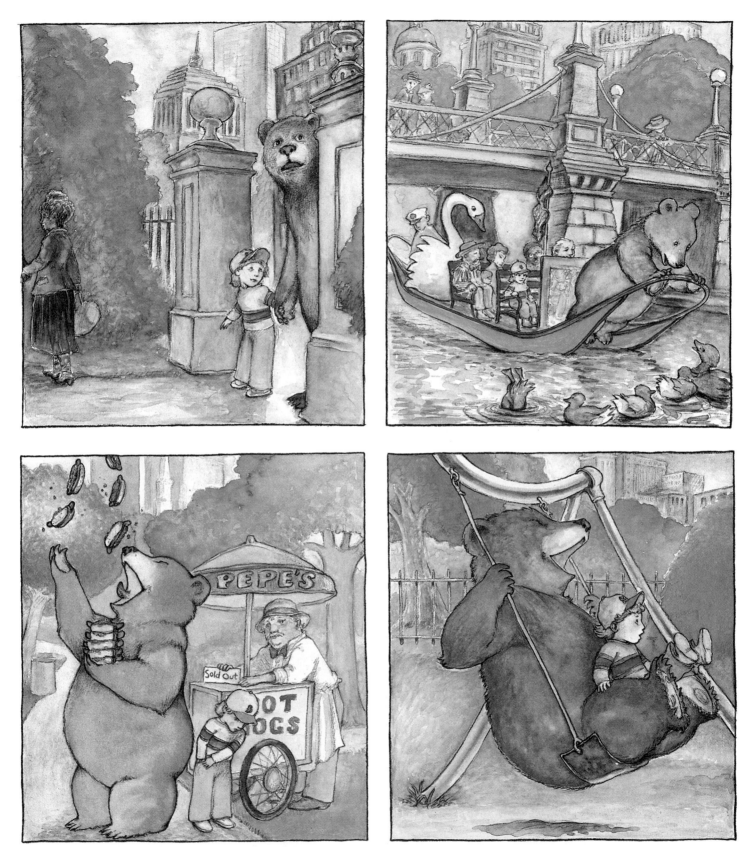

We are having a good time.

But it is getting late, and the bear is still lost.

"Let's try the library," I tell him.

"We can find out anything here!"

Inside the library we look through lots of books.

The bear sees a picture that looks like his home.

We find the place on a map and hurry outside.

A bus is leaving.

We get on the bus and ride for a long time.

Finally, we are there.

"*This* is where I live!" says the bear.

He gives me a hug and thanks me again for my help.
Then he waves good-bye and disappears into the forest.

The trees are so tall, and there aren't any people.

"Wait!" I call to the bear, "come back!"

"I think I'm lost!" I tell him.

"Don't worry," he says. "I will help you."

🐻 What did you like best about this story?

🐻 Do you think the boy was a good friend to the bear? Explain your answer.

WRITE   How will the bear help the boy find his home? Write what happens next.

DAVID McPHAIL

Words About the Author and Illustrator

David McPhail writes the words and draws the pictures for his books. He began to draw when he was two years old. He has been drawing beautiful pictures ever since.

Mr. McPhail sometimes writes about animals who act just like children. The bear in "Lost!" talks and feels just as you might feel if you were lost. Would you like to read more about a bear and a boy? Read The Bear's Toothache and First Flight by David McPhail.

Oh Where, Oh Where Has My Little Dog Gone?

illustrated by Robin Spowart

Oh where, oh where has my little dog gone?
Oh where, oh where can he be?
With his ears cut short and his tail cut long,
Oh where, oh where is he?

Jamaica's Find

Juanita Havill

Illustrations by Anne Sibley O'Brien

When Jamaica arrived at the park, there was no one there.

It was almost supper time, but she still had a few minutes to play.

She sat in a swing, pushed off with her toes, and began pumping.

It was fun not to have to watch out for the little ones who always ran in front of the swings.

Then she climbed up the slide.

There was a red sock hat on the ladder step.

Jamaica took it for a ride.

She slid down so fast that she fell in the sand and lay flat on her back.

When she rolled over to get up, she saw a stuffed dog beside her.

It was a cuddly gray dog, worn from hugging.

All over it were faded food and grass stains.

Its button nose must have fallen off.

There was a round white spot in its place.

Two black ears hung from its head.

Jamaica put the dog in her bicycle basket.
She took the hat into the park house and
gave it to the young man at the counter.

The first thing her mother said when Jamaica came in the door was: "Where did that dog come from?"

"The park. I stopped to play on the way home," Jamaica said.

"I found someone's red hat and took it to the Lost and Found."

"But, Jamaica, you should have returned the dog, too," said her mother.

Then she said, "I'm glad you returned the hat."

"It didn't fit me," Jamaica said.

"Maybe the dog doesn't fit you either," her mother said.

"I like the dog," said Jamaica.

"Don't put that silly dog on the table!"
Jamaica's brother said.

"You don't know where it came from.
It isn't very clean, you know," her father
said.

"Not in the kitchen, Jamaica," her
mother said.

Jamaica took the dog to her room. She could hear her mother say, "It probably belongs to a girl just like Jamaica."

After dessert Jamaica went to her room
very quietly.

She held the dog up and looked
at it closely.

Then she tossed it on a chair.

"Jamaica," her mother called from the kitchen. "Have you forgotten? It's your turn to dry the dishes."

"Do I have to, Mother? I don't feel good," Jamaica answered. Jamaica heard the pots rattle. Then she heard her mother's steps.

Her mother came in quietly, sat down by Jamaica, and looked at the stuffed dog, which lay alone on the chair.

She didn't say anything.

After a while she put her arms around Jamaica and squeezed for a long time.

"Mother, I want to take the dog back to the park," Jamaica said.

"We'll go first thing in the morning." Her mother smiled.

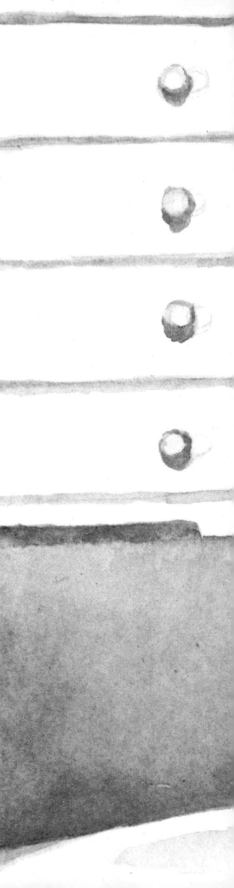

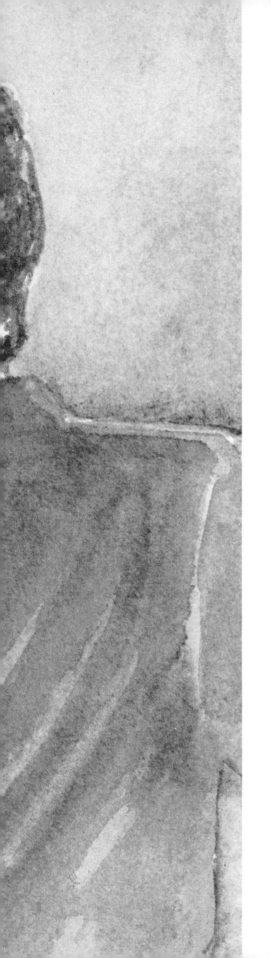

Jamaica ran to the park house and plopped the stuffed dog on the counter.

"I found this by the slide," she told the young man.

"Oh, hi. Aren't you the girl who gave me the hat last night?"

"Yes," said Jamaica, feeling hot around her ears.

"You sure do find a lot of things. I'll put it on the Lost and Found shelf."

Jamaica stood watching him.

"Is that all?" he asked. "You didn't find anything else, did you?"

"No. That's all." She stayed to watch him put the dog on a shelf behind him.

"I'm sure some little girl or boy will come in after it today, a nice little dog like that," the young man said.

Jamaica ran outside.

She didn't feel like playing alone.

There was no one else at the park but her mother, who sat on a bench.

Then Jamaica saw a girl and her mother cross the street to the park.

"Hi. I'm Jamaica. What's your name?" she
said to the girl.

The girl let go of her mother's hand.
"Kristin," she said.

"Do you want to climb the jungle gym
with me, Kristin?" Jamaica said.

Kristin ran toward Jamaica. "Yes, but I have to find something first."

"What?" asked Jamaica. Kristin was bending under the slide.

"What did you lose?" said Jamaica.

"Edgar dog. I brought him with me yesterday and now I can't find him," Kristin answered.

"Was he kind of gray with black ears?" Jamaica couldn't keep from shouting. "Come along with me."

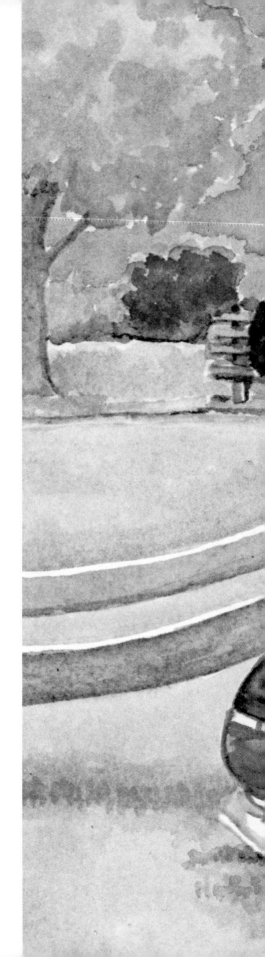

189

190

The young man in the park house looked
over the counter at the two girls.

"Now what have you found?" he asked
Jamaica.

But this time Jamaica didn't drop anything
onto the counter.

Instead, she smiled her biggest smile. "I
found the girl who belongs to that stuffed dog."

Jamaica was almost as happy as Kristin,
who took Edgar dog in her arms and gave
him a big welcome-back hug.

🐕 How did you feel when Jamaica returned
the dog?

🐕 What lesson did Jamaica learn?

WRITE   Imagine that you are Kristin. Write a
thank-you note to Jamaica.

Lost and Found

Imagine that Jamaica found the bear in "Lost!" What do you think she would have done?

What would you have done if you were the child in one of the stories?

WRITER'S WORKSHOP

Did you ever find something special? What did you do with it? Write a letter to Jamaica. Tell her about it.

CONNECTIONS

Multicultural Connection

Jo Ann Jeong

When Jo Ann Jeong was a girl, she visited a forest with her class. A park ranger told the children about the plants and animals in the forest. Jo Ann thought to herself, "What a great job!"

Jo Ann Jeong never forgot that field trip. When she grew up, she became a park ranger for Golden Gate National Recreation Area in California.

Write about the job of a park ranger. Tell why this job might be fun.

Social Studies Connection

A Great Job for Me

Think of a time when you said to yourself, "What a great job!" What job would you like to have someday? On a sheet of paper, write about your dream job. Draw a picture of yourself working at that job.

Geography Connection

National Parks

Get a book about national parks from the library. What is special about each park? Which park would you like to see? Make a travel poster for a national park. Draw some special things you would see there.

GLOSSARY

A

across   Travis and his dad sailed **across** the river.

again   Mark swam in the morning and **again** after lunch.

almost   The sun was going down, so it was **almost** night.

alone   Leon was with me, so I was not **alone**.

also   Put on your left shoe **also**.

animals   Cows and pigs are farm **animals**.

animals

B

because   I laughed at the joke **because** it was funny.

believe   Jan does not **believe** that ants can talk.

blue   Our flag is red, white, and **blue**.

books   I like to read **books** about birds.

books

C

car   Use your seat belt in the **car.**

careful   Be **careful** when crossing the street.

city   There are many cars and people in a **city.**

clock   A **clock** shows us what time it is.

close   Rick lives so **close** to school that he can walk.

clock

D

dinner   My dad cooked **dinner** for us.

E

else   I want something **else** to eat.

enough   I am old **enough** to ride a bike.

even   I **even** cleaned under the bed.

eyes   You cannot see me with your **eyes** closed.

eyes

F

far   The ball landed **far** away.

few   I have only a **few** pennies.

flower   The red **flower** grew by the tree.

found   Melinda lost her cat, but I **found** it.

fruit   Oranges and apples are **fruit.**

few

G

garage   The new car is in the **garage.**

glows   The firefly **glows** in the dark.

gone   Jeff has **gone** to the beach.

gray   The clouds were **gray** before it rained.

great   We had a **great** time on the boat.

growing   The baby is **growing** fast.

gray

H

head　　You wear a hat on your **head.**

hear　　Did you **hear** a dog bark?

himself　　Joel can tie his shoes by **himself.**

his　　All **his** new toys are in the basket.

hurt　　Kim fell down and **hurt** her leg.

head

I

idea　　Mario had the best **idea** for how to make a kite.

K

knew　　Peter **knew** all about lions.

idea

L

later　　Let's play now and pick up our toys **later.**

lay　　I **lay** on the grass and looked up at the sky.

leave　　I will **leave** my muddy shoes outside.

long　　It took Rob a **long** time to walk home.

lay

N

never   **Never** mind. I'll clean up the mess later.

O

or   We can play inside, **or** we can play outside.

other   She is in the **other** room.

P

paper   Tonya made a hat out of **paper**.

park   Trees and grass grow all over the **park**.

peace   Mom wants **peace** and quiet when she is sleeping.

people   Many **people** went to the show.

picture   I can draw a **picture** of a cow.

pointing   The teacher was **pointing** to a word.

pretty   The flowers are very **pretty**.

paper

R

rain   Her bike got wet in the **rain**.

room   My toys and bed are in my **room**.

rain

S

scare   You will **scare** the baby with that toy.

school   We read and write at **school.**

seeds   Apple trees grow from apple **seeds.**

sky   From my window I can see the blue **sky.**

sleep   At night we **sleep** in our beds.

sleeve   Put your arm in the **sleeve** of your coat.

smiled   Ben **smiled** because he was happy.

snow   We played outside in the **snow.**

stairs   I go up the **stairs** to get to my room.

star   I looked up and saw a **star** in the sky.

started   Rita opened the book and **started** to read.

stood   Jackie sat down, and then she **stood** up.

story   The teacher read a **story** about a frog.

street   We saw the bus coming up the **street.**

such   We had **such** a good time swimming.

sure   She **sure** can run fast!

surprise   It was a big **surprise** to get my own dog.

sky

smiled

star

T

talk   I will **talk** to Terrence about his trip.

them   Let's tell **them** about the party.

thought   Liz **thought** the game was silly.

tired   Eric was so **tired** that he took a nap.

turning   The leaves were falling and **turning** in the wind.

tweet   **Tweet** is a sound that birds make.

talk

U

under   Our dog sleeps **under** my bed.

until   We will stay inside **until** the rain stops.

used   They **used** bricks to build a house.

under

W

while   We sat on the steps for a little **while.**

won't   Karen is sick, so she **won't** be at the party.